This Doodle By Number
Belongs To

....

By Doodle Lovely

Within you, there is a stillness and a sanctuary to which you can retreat at any time and be yourself.

HERMANN HESSE

www.DoodleLovely.com

MEOW!

Or, as we non-feline critters would say, 'HELLO!'

Doodle By Number™ isn't just for kids, it's for anyone who wants to quiet their busy thoughts, awaken their creative spirit and enjoy the peace that comes with a little mindfulness.

And who better to guide us through a mindful activity than the master of mindfulness, ruler of reverie, captain of contemplation and curious contemplator, our fluffy friend, the cat.

Cats are pros at slowing things down, making themselves comfortable and reveling in quiet contemplation.

That's why I designed this book: cats and doodling are a natural fit, and we could all benefit from more of both.

You don't need to be an artist or an expert to enjoy doodling. You just need to start moving your pen across the paper, ready to follow the journey wherever it may lead.

Wishing you a cat-tastic day of doodles,

Melissa x

WHY DOODLE?

It's true! People have been doodling for millennia.
"Spontaneous drawing" has been studied and verified as a
means to decrease stress in our lives.

Taking pen in hand and using the rhythmic motions of doodling, activates
the relaxation response within the brain. Just the thing to calm the chaos!

Playfulness
Doodling promotes
well-being, allowing you to
lighten your mood whenever
you feel overwhelmed.

Creative Freedom
Doodling is a workout
for the mind that can help
you focus on new ideas and
bring fresh insights.

Improved Focus
Doodling is a simple and
effective way to help you
concentrate and process
information.

DISCOVER
THE BENEFITS
OF DOODLING
TODAY

Manage Emotions
Doodling is a safe method
to evaluate unsettling
emotions, converting jumbled
feelings into a peaceful
state of mind.

Greater Productivity
Doodling can refresh your
mind and reset your thoughts,
allowing for a greater
sense of clarity.

Increased Memory
Studies indicate that while
listening to others, the brain
can recall 29% more
information while doodling.

How to use your

DOODLE *by* NUMBER™

Pick up a pen, your favorite marker, or pencil of any color.

At the bottom of each example page there is a selection
of five doodle patterns to choose from. Each pattern is
circled and numbered.

Follow the numbers to create a doodle pattern on the
opposite page. If you want to use more or less doodles,
go for it!

Complete the *Doodle By Number*™ and touch it up
to your satisfaction.

Feel free to make the doodle your own with your
favorite shapes, lines and patterns. Even add color if you like.
Doodle-riffic!

Follow the numbers to match your doodles on the opposite page.

1 - Paw Circles   2 - Tents   3 - Scallop & Circles   4 - Lines   5 - Scallops

Be happy
in the moment,
that's enough.
Each moment
is all we need,
no more.

MOTHER TERESA

Follow the numbers to match your doodles on the opposite page.

1 - Zig Zags & Lines   2 - Loops   3 - Puffs   4 - Wavy Lines   5 - Circles

Learning never exhausts the mind.

LEONARDO DA VINCI

Follow the numbers to match your doodles on the opposite page.

1 - Triangles

2 - Branches

3 - Wavy Lines

4 - Circles & Strokes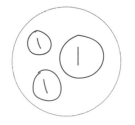

5 - Lines

Beauty is how you feel inside, and it reflects in your eyes. It is not something physical.

SOPHIA LOREN

Follow the numbers to match your doodles on the opposite page.

1 - Wavy Lines	2 - Mini Rainbows	3 - Short Lines	4 - W's	5 - Lines

If you don't
live your life,
then who will?

RIHANNA

Follow the numbers to match your doodles on the opposite page.

1 - Swirls & Circles	2 - Double S's	3 - Triangles	4 - U's	5 - Lines

  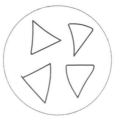  

To love oneself
is the beginning of a
lifelong romance.

OSCAR WILDE

TREATS

FLOUR

Follow the numbers to match your doodles on the opposite page.

1 - Mini Rainbows

2 - Florals

3 - W's

4 - Lines & Dots

5 - Weaving

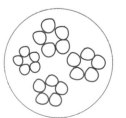

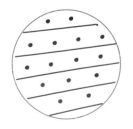

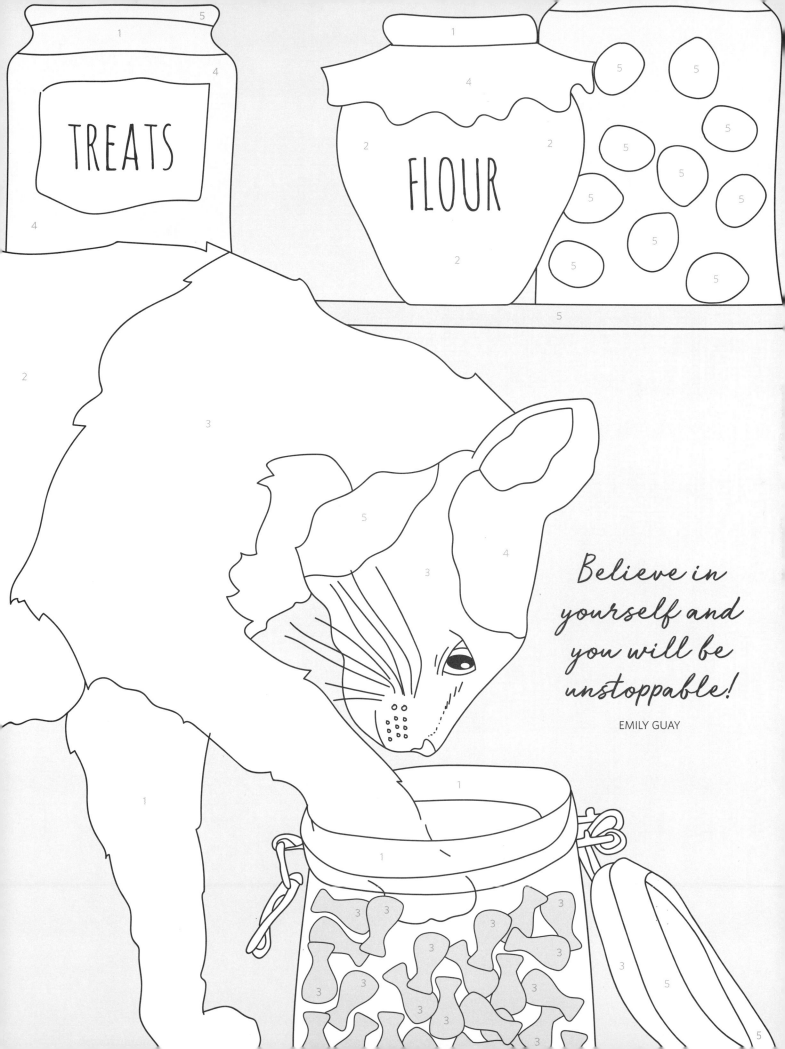

Believe in
yourself and
you will be
unstoppable!

EMILY GUAY

Follow the numbers to match your doodles on the opposite page.

1 - Circles   2 - Triangles & Circles   3 - Circles & Dots   4 - Double Squiggles   5 - Lines

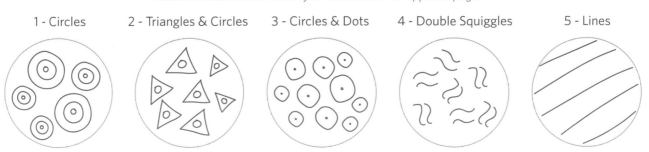

If you want the rainbow, you gotta put up with the rain.

DOLLY PARTON

Follow the numbers to match your doodles on the opposite page.

1 - Retro Drops   2 - Stars   3 - Cross Hatch   4 - Lines & Circles   5 - Scallops

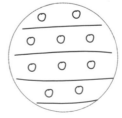

Nothing is a waste of time if you
use the experience wisely.

AUGUSTE RODIN

Follow the numbers to match your doodles on the opposite page.

1 - Sprouts

2 - Dotted Lines

3 - Swirls

4 - Wickets

5 - Wood Grain

Today...spend more time with
people who bring out the best in you,
not the stress in you.

UNKNOWN

Follow the numbers to match your doodles on the opposite page.

1 - Lines & Circles   2 - Sparks   3 - Drops   4 - Sprouts   5 - Spirals

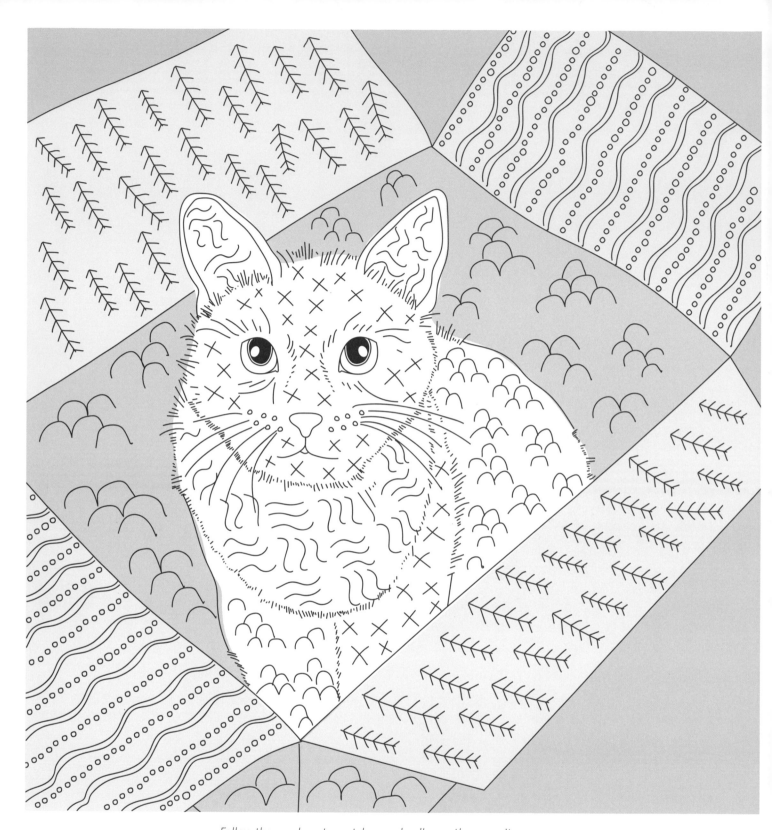

Follow the numbers to match your doodles on the opposite page.

1 - X's   2 - Fish Bones   3 - Scallops   4 - Wavy Print   5 - Cross Hatch

The challenge is not to be perfect – it is to be whole.

JANE FONDA

Follow the numbers to match your doodles on the opposite page.

1 - Fuzzy Seed   2 - Leaf Imprint   3 - Circles   4 - Fork Tops   5 - Wood Grain

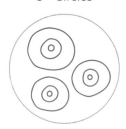

Smile, breathe
and go slowly.
THICH NHÂT HANH

Follow the numbers to match your doodles on the opposite page.

1 - Flowers   2 - Buds   3 - Leaves   4 - Dashes   5 - Loops

Slow down and enjoy the simple pleasures in life.

UNKNOWN

Follow the numbers to match your doodles on the opposite page.

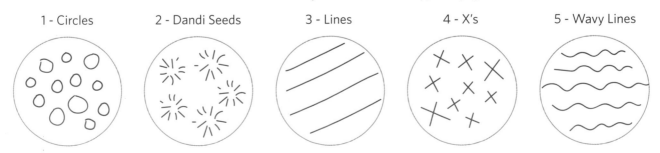

1 - Circles   2 - Dandi Seeds   3 - Lines   4 - X's   5 - Wavy Lines

Wherever life
plants you, bloom
with grace.

UNKNOWN

Follow the numbers to match your doodles on the opposite page.

1 - Snowflake 1   2 - Snowflake 2   3 - Zig Zags   4 - Puffs   5 - Circles

Almost everything will work again if you unplug it for a few minutes, including you.

ANNE LAMOT

Follow the numbers to match your doodles on the opposite page.

1 - Circles   2 - Sprinkles   3 - Loops   4 - X's   5 - Lines

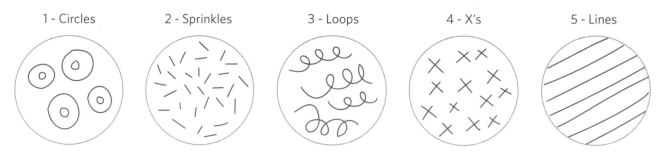

The beginning is always today.

MARY WOLLSTONECRAFT

Follow the numbers to match your doodles on the opposite page.

1 - Florals   2 - Buds   3 - L's   4 - Circles   5 - Fans

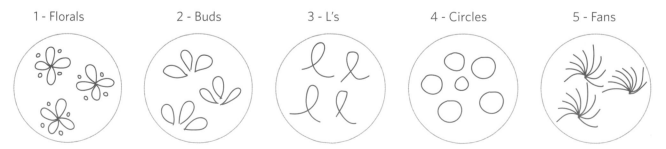

I truly believe that the privilege of a lifetime is being who you are.

VIOLA DAVIS

Follow the numbers to match your doodles on the opposite page.

1 - Striped Pod

2 - Buds

3 - Swirls

4 - Star Bursts

5 - Zig Zags

Find something that makes
you happy and go for it.

ZENDAYA

Follow the numbers to match your doodles on the opposite page.

1 - Waves

2 - Repetitive Lines

3 - Cloud Line

4 - Peaks

5 - Swirls

We cannot direct the wind, but we can adjust the sails.

DOLLY PARTON

Follow the numbers to match your doodles on the opposite page.

1 - Floral 1   2 - Floral 2   3 - Swirls   4 - Wavy Lines   5 - Power Polls

No act
of kindness,
no matter
how small,
is ever wasted.

AESOP

Follow the numbers to match your doodles on the opposite page.

1 - Stars 2 - Zig Zags 3 - Puffs 4 - Arches & Dots 5 - Hatching

Life isn't about finding yourself. Life is about creating yourself.

GEORGE BERNARD SHAW

Follow the numbers to match your doodles on the opposite page.

1 - Suns   2 - Bursts   3 - Florals   4 - Tents   5 - Herringbone

If you stumble, make it part of the dance.

MARK TWAIN

Follow the numbers to match your doodles on the opposite page.

1 - Diamonds & Circles   2 - Loops   3 - Swirl Bursts   4 - Bumps   5 - Sprinkles

 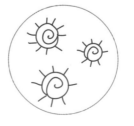   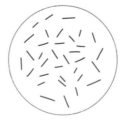

The best therapist
has four legs.

UNKNOWN

Follow the numbers to match your doodles on the opposite page.

| 1 - Scallops | 2 -X's | 3 - Zig Zags | 4 - Circles | 5 - Lines |

We don't stop
playing because
we grow old;
we grow old because
we stop playing.

GEORGE BERNARD SHAW

Follow the numbers to match your doodles on the opposite page.

1 - Scallop Trim

2 - Stars

3 - Sprouts

4 -Florals

5 - Wavy Lines

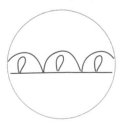

Don't let anyone tell you
that you have to be a certain way.
Be unique. Be what you feel.

MELISSA ETHERIDGE

Follow the numbers to match your doodles on the opposite page.

1 - Puffs 2 - Wavy Lines 3 - Tents 4 - Leaves 5 - Lines

There are always flowers for
those who want to see them.

HENRI MATISSE

Follow the numbers to match your doodles on the opposite page.

1 - Stars	2 - Sprinkles	3 - Lines	4 - Circles	5 - Zig Zags

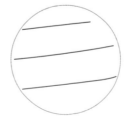

You have to nourish to flourish.

UNKNOWN

Follow the numbers to match your doodles on the opposite page.

1 - Track 　2 - Floral Circles 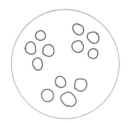　3 - Double C's 　4 - Line Bursts 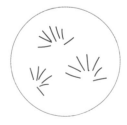　5 - Short Lines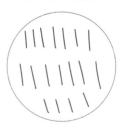

Follow the numbers to match your doodles on the opposite page.

1 - Swirls & Circles   2 - Fan Lines   3 - Cross Hatch   4 - Pyramids   5 - Star Bursts

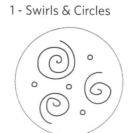

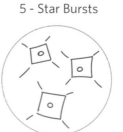

All we have is today.
Just live it. We don't
know about tomorrow.
So, enjoy the day.
Love yourself and spread
love around.

CHARLOTTE RAE

Follow the numbers to match your doodles on the opposite page.

1 - Swirls & Circles   2 - Triangle Pattern   3 - Circle Bursts   4 - Puffs   5 - Lines

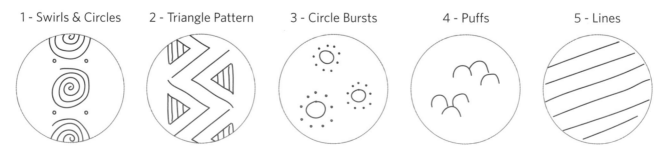

It's not selfish
to love yourself,
take care of yourself
and to make your
happiness a priority.
It's necessary.

MANDY HALE

Meet the Doodler

MELISSA LLOYD is an international doodler, designer,
teacher, author and inspirationalist. Her passion for
creativity can be found globally on products, environments
and in the hearts of those with whom she has connected.

Melissa combines her twenty plus years of experience
in professional design and communication with her passion
for humanity, psychology, art therapy and mindfulness;
infusing a deep understanding of self.

Melissa teaches soul-care through creative practices and
encourages you to learn how to navigate the stormy seas of life,
reducing stress and rejuvenating your mind.

By honouring your creative soul and the celebration of
living in the moment, Melissa inspires you to bring joy back
into your life by finding a place of peace internally.
Her transformational approach to creativity, through doodling
and living, inspires others to live a healthier and happier life.
'Always Be You... For You.'

Melissa balances her time between mothering, creating,
teaching and living in her little Cottage By The Sea.
To discover more of Melissa's work visit: **DoodleLovely.com**

Be you, for you.

(Rinse & Repeat)

Did you enjoy this *Doodle By Number*™? We would love to hear your feedback!
Please email us: **hello@doodlelovely.com**

Connect with us to know when the next edition of *Doodle By Number*™
will be available in our online shop.
www.DoodleLovely.com